WRITERS

ON

WRITERS

Published in partnership with

WRITERS
ALICE
PUNG
ON
JOHN
MARSDEN
WRITERS

Black Inc.

Published by Black Inc.
in association with the University of Melbourne and State Library Victoria.

Black Inc., an imprint of Schwartz Publishing Pty Ltd
Level 1, 221 Drummond Street, Carlton VIC 3053, Australia
enquiries@blackincbooks.com • www.blackincbooks.com

State Library Victoria
328 Swanston Street, Melbourne VIC 3000, Australia
www.slv.vic.gov.au

The University of Melbourne
Parkville VIC 3010, Australia
www.unimelb.edu.au

National Library of Australia Cataloguing-in-Publication entry:
Pung, Alice, author.
On John Marsden / Alice Pung.
9781863959568 (hardback)
9781925435726 (ebook)
Marsden, John, 1950 – Influence.
Authors, Australian – 20th century – Biography.
Young adult fiction – Authorship.
Fiction – Authorship.

Cover and text design by Peter Long
Photograph of Alice Pung: Federica Roselli
Photograph of John Marsden: Stuart McEvoy/Newspix

Printed in China by 1010 International.

'We kill all the caterpillars,
then complain there are no butterflies.'

The Dead of the Night

Dear John,

The first time it occurred to me that you were a real person was the morning my friend Angela came to school and said, 'You'll never believe what happened. We bumped into John Marsden.'

'Nooo way!'

To us, you weren't real, and if you were, you weren't someone who'd be loitering in the western suburbs of Melbourne. But Angela meant it literally: her mum had bashed her car into yours somewhere down the Tullamarine Freeway, and you were so kind about it you even gave them some of your books.

We all knew *of* you, but not *about* you. We studied *So Much to Tell You* during the first term of Year 9 at Christ the King College. Our parents had sent us to the Catholic school in Braybrook to save us from temptation. Fortressed by a wall of carpet factories and sequestered next to a nunnery, we studied in an oasis of industry and restraint in one of the roughest neighbourhoods in Victoria. In primary school, when one boy fractured another boy's wrist, my best friend spent all lunchtime trying to convince the victim not to dob on her brother. Another of my ten-year-old friends saw the counsellor every week because her stepfather kept 'mucking around' with her. One recess, the boys from the technical college just over the fence from our school found a bird with a broken wing, brought it to the Preps and then snapped its neck in front of them. We called kids 'bin scabs' if at lunchtime they yanked food out of bins to eat, because we thought that was a normal quirk of childhood, a habit no different to picking actual scabs – disgusting, but not a sign of any larger tragedy, like not having enough food at home.

This is all a bit bleak, isn't it? Maybe I should have started by hailing the heroic females in your novels, and how they gave me girl power. But that would be a lie because the characters in your novels I most identify with are not 'heroic', nor are they always female. I could mention your children's picture book *Millie*, to soften things up a bit for the reader. But, John, even your children's books piss people off! 'Millie is an odious, conniving, lying child, who gets away with all her hideous behaviour,' writes one reviewer. 'Even when she's caught in the act everyone just says "we all love Millie"? Oh please.' Millie's transgressions include brushing her dog's teeth with her own toothbrush and resourcefully hiding everything under the bed when asked to tidy up.

I guess the problem with your stories is that you don't include the punishment at the end.

In high school a friend was reading *The Dead of the Night*, and our science teacher wryly remarked, as he looked at the back cover, 'I presume this will be filled with violence and sex and the usual teenage preoccupations.' Yes, it was, and yes, we were very preoccupied with them. We thought they were far more fascinating than the usual 'adult themes' that people around us were constantly discussing: overtime, tax and rent.

Your books appealed to us because they made our experiences central. Children and young adults often don't have the words to describe what is going on inside them. Even when they do, their stories are translated and interpreted by adults in a way that bears scant resemblance to lived experience. But you kept it real, so real that even your first publisher, Walter McVitty, who took such a risk on *So Much to Tell You*, felt ambivalent about your later books:

> To have turned so many children on to reading is a wonderful thing to have achieved, I think. And yet, if I was asked, would I like my little grandchildren to be exposed to those books, maybe I would say no. I just feel that the mind of a young person is such a malleable thing, I would want them to grow up in as uncorrupted a world as possible. I don't feel as though I want to be rubbing my children's noses in it.

I wonder what you are rubbing children's noses in? Could it be Australia's colonial history (*The Rabbits*), the effect of political corruption on families (*Checkers*), the loneliness of juvenile detention, or the terror of not having your abuse taken seriously (*Letters from the Inside*)? Maybe it's the inordinate blind rage of being from a poor background with no real life prospects, and on top of that dealing with a disability (*Dear Miffy*), or the effects of wartime post-traumatic stress (the *Tomorrow* series)?

You once pointed out that childhood and adolescence are when a person has the most number of first experiences, and perhaps that's what people mean when they say that the young are 'impressionable'. But then you added, 'If you've ever tried to persuade a three-year-old to eat spinach you'll soon see how impressionable they are.' And you mentioned that plenty of adults are impressionable – Hitler, Pol Pot and Jim Jones had no trouble finding disciples among the old and middle-aged.

Much of the time, I reckon stories about children are an 'adults-only' fantasy of childhood, revealing more about the writer and their projections than the truth of their subjects. In 1992, Susan Orlean wrote her famous profile for *Esquire*, 'The American Male at Age Ten', which now reads like an early '90s list of a ten-year-old boy's consumer preferences – Morgan Freeman movies, Nintendo, *Streetfighter II*. It begins, 'If Colin Duffy and I were to get married, we would have matching superhero notebooks … We would eat pizza and candy for all of our meals. We wouldn't have sex, but we would have crushes on each other and, magically, babies would appear in our home.'

The piece was groundbreaking because it was the first time a famous international magazine had published a piece about the interests of an 'ordinary' kid that was written with the same focus of intensity and analysis as an interview with the president. But to me, reading it now, it really grates, especially when Orlean observes: 'That ten-year-olds feel the weight of the world and consider it their mission to shoulder it came as a surprise to me.' What world is she living in? Apparently a world where 'Colin loves recycling. He loves it even more than, say, playing with little birds.'

Perhaps it's those who are charmed by stories like Colin Duffy's, seeing them as signs that our future is in 'good' hands, who have the most trouble with your books, John. Your fiercest critics are probably those who have the luxury of thinking that childhood should be free of anxiety, worry, sadness, illness, stress and grief – emotions that every child feels at some point or another. You once said about *Letters from the Inside*: 'I was struck, as I have been many times since, by the fact that young readers react so differently to older readers, but older readers don't seem to notice that.'

I remember enlightened school librarians recommending books by Robin Klein, Sonya Hartnett, Melina Marchetta, Cynthia Voigt, Robert Cormier and Paul Zindel. Each of their works examined darkness, morality and death. This was beautiful and clear writing from literary artists who asked more questions than they answered. Later, young adult books devolved into 'single-problem novels' – divorce, drug abuse, assault, incest – and I grew tired of formulaic stories whose serious themes and tidy 'lessons' could not mask their uninspired prose and blunt commercial salaciousness.

What you manage to capture in your writing is an authentic Australian child's voice. Your boys in *Staying Alive in Year 5* and *The Year My*

Life Broke are not adult projections of cuteness, but autonomous human beings:

> My first day I sat next to a kid called Nirvana … he only spoke three words to me all morning. 'Yeah', 'no', 'dunno', that was it. At recess he nicked off to play cricket. I wanted to follow him but I also didn't want to look desperate, so I ended up going in a different direction.

This might read as prosaic to an adult reader more accustomed to the endearing ways of precocious opinionators, yet this boy has agency, suffers awkwardness and indecision, and doesn't have an arsenal of words with which to combat loneliness.

One of my primary-school friends, who was Colin Duffy's age, bragged that his outworker parents paid him ten cents for every shirt collar he ironed. His plan was to iron a hundred shirt collars in a week, so that by Friday he would have ten dollars and buy the canteen's supply of lollies. Here was a man with agency and purpose! On Dave's glorious payday, kids waited at the school gate for him to turn up with his pockets full of coins. But when he arrived he just glowered and walked straight past them. Later, everyone realised that he was also the *only dry kid*, because his practical Chinese-Cambodian mother had made him buy a 'friggin' umbrella' with his week's earnings!

When Orlean was interviewed in 2014 about Duffy, she said, 'I really grew to adore this kid. He was just enchanting … utterly entrancing … I felt so charmed … caught up in this magical world.' Bogan kids are never described as 'utterly entrancing'; and bogan Asian kids don't exist in literature except in tragic reports about garage-sewing, where they have horrible accidents getting their arms caught in sewing machines.

Maybe we like to infantilise children – in books and in life – because we believe they are filled with the 'goodness' we've inculcated in them, and god forbid this innocence should ever be tainted by experience. Rachel Cusk writes about the way children are characters in the family story we tell ourselves:

> Until adolescence, parents by and large control the family story. The children are the subject of this story, sure enough, the generators of its interest or charm, but they remain, as it were, characters … A large part of parental authority is invested in the maintenance and upkeep of this story, its repetition, its continued iterations and adaptations.

But these subjects inevitably grow up to learn about the arbitrary nature of the world outside the Parental Kingdom. Rusalka, a teenager on Goodreads, reviewed *Dear Miffy* and came to this conclusion:

> [It made] me realise that my non-romantic way of experiencing the world was not because my experience was broken, but [that] kids fiction was. Adult life can not be romantic and beautiful. This book helped me deal with that. While it sounds horrible as a review, to me personally, from my heart, I could not give it a better one.

Our Year 9 teacher, Ms Bonnie Clarke, didn't make us analyse *So Much to Tell You* for 'themes', but in her class we could discuss important things without talking about them directly.

There was none of the pressure there would be in front of a school counsellor. She made each of us pick a character from your book and create a monologue in their voice. I typed a histrionic speech in the 'voice' of Marina's mother onto sheets of tissue paper and fake-cried my way through the presentation. Carol did a smart-arse, true-to-character rendition of Sophie, saying of Marina's half-scarred face: 'She could do a one-woman show of *Beauty and the Beast*, just by turning the other cheek.'

So Much to Tell You might come with trigger warnings in some schools today, but back when I was fourteen it helped us understand the intricate clockwork of different families. We were cheery and resilient girls, but one friend always came to school bleary-eyed and often dozed at her desk because she'd spent too many late nights working in her parents' garage. Another experienced a death in the family on her fifteenth birthday. A third would not live past her twenties.

Yet Year 9 was the last year I studied young adult fiction at school. The following year, I was at a new school, in a blazer for the first time, studying Henry James and Charles Dickens. I learned to appreciate the literary grandeur of these works, but never once did it occur to me that I could relate them to my own life. No one told me that was what literature was for. My intellectual life had become theoretical and complex, while my real life of looking after younger siblings and housework, speaking another language at home and existing in a different, frozen-in-time culture, working at my dad's electrical appliance store, navigating the intensity of teen friendships – none of this other complexity had a place in our school curriculum.

Never again did I feel so validated as a teenage girl as when I was fourteen. Never again would our stories be so central.

Teenagers have unimaginable power, and maybe this is one of the reasons we are so afraid of them. Suddenly, an adolescent finds herself capable of breaking down what Cusk calls the 'twin fortresses' of adult control: verbal and physical superiority. The narrative of good versus evil that some parents maintain for their children against, or at the expense of, all lived experience (Hobbesian schoolyards, imperfect families, or surprising generosity from that one 'feral' kid you're meant to keep away from) is now suspect. Suddenly, a parent can no longer dictate the friends their children are 'allowed' to have, the places they can be or the experiences they might encounter.

By the time I finished Year 12, I had been to

five different schools. In each new place, I met girls who secretly gloated about their power of having knowledge over adults. One girl lost her virginity in the darkness of a cinema. Another lost her sanity because her father had pressured her into studying only maths-and-science-related subjects in which she failed time and again. A friend at university read *Harry Potter* in secret because her mother thought it was inspired by the occult. Love, knowledge, self-expression – these were things we sought as young adults, but did not trust the adult world to understand, let alone provide.

The rather pure motivations of my friends could be distilled into these one-sentence summaries:

The first time you have sex has to be special.
I work as hard as I can.

I'm curious about this book and would like to decide for myself.

Yet our actions were complicated and corrupted by secrecy and subterfuge, which we believed were necessary to subdue the anxieties of adults. You understand that 'first experiences can push you in different directions, even directions that surprise you'. What a teenager wants is to have these experiences *acknowledged*, not explained or judged. Cusk identifies that a lot of conflict between adolescents and adults has to do with the freedom we grant teenagers to tell their own stories: 'I wonder how much of what we call conflict is in fact our own deserved punishment for telling the story wrong, for twisting it with our own vanity or wishful thinking, for failing to honour the truth.'

You appreciate that much of young people's frustration stems from the inability of adults to separate love from control, or distinguish honesty from over-protection: 'telling lies to anyone is wrong … No one has the right to decide on behalf of someone else what they should or shouldn't be allowed to know. Your right to the truth takes precedence over adults' right to keep you in ignorance.'

The teenagers in your books go to prison, mental institutions and war; have sex; run their deceased parents' estates; inadvertently get caught up in political scandals; experience domestic violence; rob, assault and kill. They also see and experience unspeakable things, rendering them wordless.

A healthy, safe child will be open to talking about their lives and interests, and will even be happy to be profiled for a magazine. They have nothing to hide. A child from an economically, socially or politically disadvantaged background, a child of trauma, a young person with a mental illness – they have plenty to hide, and they learn to hide it quick-smart because even when they find stories reflecting their experiences, their parents or teachers might tell them these stories are overhyped, or 'bad influences', or don't belong in the higher echelons of serious 'literature'.

Yet when we want children to learn compassion for refugees, we don't take them to the neighbouring suburbs to meet real refugees. We make them read a book or watch a movie. I am asked to give talks to schools about the killing fields of Cambodia, but am often warned beforehand not to make it 'too traumatic for our girls, please'. I'm supposed to spread an anti-war message, but spare the details; to convey a triumph-over-adversity narrative. While I was writing my book about my father, even he asked, 'Maybe there's too much suffering in here? White people don't want to read *too much* suffering.'

But *reading is never the same as experiencing*.

From a very young age, around eight, we had family film nights whenever war movies – *Apocalypse Now, The Killing Fields, Heaven & Earth* – were on television. My brother and I could block our eyes during certain scenes if we wanted, but no adult blocked the violence onscreen for us. My dad always said, 'Don't worry, this is just a movie. There's nothing to fear. We experienced the real thing and it was much, much worse.' Watching my parents happily shelling peanuts, I remember feeling safe and loved, connected to such a stoic and resilient history. I also remember feeling smug the next day, when kids at school would play war games inspired by the movies. Even as they shot at us, the 'gooks', we didn't care. They were just kids with fake finger-guns whose parents had never travelled further than Mildura. We were the real deal.

We applaud children from good neighbourhoods who can engage in delicate debates about female genital mutilation and cultural relativism, but overlook rural ones from Woop Woop who deal hands-on with sheep's dags. You said that, 'I think we're going to end up with a generation of frightened people, but also people who are emotionally and spiritually stunted by being so careful that they never get out there and try anything adventurous.'

Adolescents with an enormous capacity for hard work are the pivotal characters in your *Tomorrow* series, and you write about how they were based on students you'd taught at Geelong Grammar:

At home they drove vehicles, ploughed fields, helped with shearing and harvesting and calving and lambing – and then went to boarding schools, where they were not trusted to change a light globe or put a Band-Aid on a cut. The contrast between these two dimensions of their lives was extraordinary, and it is to their credit that most of them handled it as well as they did, although for a number it resulted in frustration and anger.

The 'terrible teens' to you, John, doesn't mean what it does to most: for you it is not something inflicted on hapless adults, but a phase of life when a burgeoning and bewildered young adult feels beset by a society that often gives them no clear guidance on how to emerge into adulthood. Given the choice, most teenagers would never depict themselves as helpless schmucks in their own lives. But of course, most teenagers have no idea of their own power:

> If the bull had wanted to smash through the fence he could have done so any time, but luckily nearly all cattle live and die without learning that. It's like school, most students go from kindergarten to Year 12 without noticing that they could do a fair amount of damage if they wanted to. They stay inside the fence.

The simple act of staying inside the fence is a problem for many characters in your books – this is where their struggle begins. Whether the fence is supposed to keep an adolescent safe (hospital), to prepare them for bigger pastures (school), or to punish (jail) will determine how willing they are to stay within its bounds. Sometimes this fence is knocked down by circumstances beyond the characters' control (war) or it is non-existent (no living parents to set boundaries).

In your ideal world, the fence would not be necessary. One of your most beautiful and lyrical books, *The Journey,* documents a fictional adolescent rite of passage into adulthood. Influenced by Hermann Hesse's *Siddhartha,* the novel sees Argus set out on a journey towards manhood. During his travels, he must collect stories and return to tell them to his community elders. Argus's parents grieve his departure, yet understand the necessity of it. On his way, Argus encounters a dead woman and a young girl in labour, leading to a birth in which he lends assistance. He finally returns home, having come into his prime, to notice that his parents have aged. Argus's realisation echoes the Buddha's discovery that people become sick, grow old and die. It is only through being responsible for other human beings – having a young family of his own – that Argus understands the fallibility of his parents:

It suddenly struck him that parents had always seemed to be so calm and unafraid, whatever the situation, and yet here they were, Jessie's parents, feeling all the emotions that he had associated only with childhood. Argus began to wonder at the apparent strength of parents. How real was it?

Not all adults are as enlightened as Argus's parents, and not all societies so focused on supporting an adolescent's coming of age. Aung San Suu Kyi said that it is not power that corrupts, but fear – fear of losing the power you have, and fear of being subject to the scourge of power. Because parental power is so complicated and so fraught with love, so burdened with pre-existing notions of 'for your own good', we don't like to acknowledge that this power can also squash an emerging adult. Winter reflects on how such relationships can cast long shadows over one's life:

> [My mother] was so obviously a powerful personality, and I knew from watching my school friends that sometimes a mother like that can overrun you. I'd seen quite a few families with powerful parents and passive kids. Like, there was only so much room in the family, and the parents took most of it.

What makes your books resonate with young adults is your understanding of the complete powerlessness they feel at times, and you situate their feelings in their wider familial, social and political circumstances. There is a miserable-hilarious scene in *Letters from the Inside* depicting petty tyranny at its most egregious. A girl in prison answers 'Yeah' instead of 'Present' at rollcall.

Mrs Neumann snapped. 'Right, you're charged: attempting to escape.' 'What?' said Jenelle. 'Yes,' said Mrs Neumann, frothing at the mouth. 'You didn't answer your name correctly, therefore you're not here. And if you're not here, you must be in Med Unit or attempting to escape.

Surely this must be made up, but no, you witnessed this very scene during your week in Risdon Prison – two adults, angry over their lack of power, making a childish scene about semantics. Words were the only weapons the weaker party had left, and the passage reminded me of a line from Ecclesiastes about how there was no one to comfort the oppressed because there was no one to comfort the oppressors.

Only in the state of powerlessness do 'childish' traits emerge in both adults and children. In my favourite novel of yours, *Dear Miffy*, Tony knows this too well:

I love it how they call it an 'attitude problem' just because you don't want to spend the best years of your life sitting in a straight line, talking in a straight line, walking in a straight line. Just because you don't want to do what they want you to do. And then they try to tell you that you're the one who's sick.

Tony is an archetypal 'scary teen', the sort that turns up in news stories in a decade's time having done some real bad shit. He comes from, as you say, 'the subculture of some young men and women from tough suburbs in big cities, who dress and act and talk in a way that people from more conservative areas find deeply threatening'.

Conservatism is a luxury sometimes – continuity, dinners at the table, a certain narrative about life that a teenager can accept or reject. Teens like Tony don't understand this story structure because their parents' lives lack narrative; their families' lives lack cohesion. In his work, my friend Les Twentyman deals with families into their third generation of welfare dependency. 'How can you ask a kid to pull their socks up when they have no socks to pull up?' he often rails, meaning: how can a person judge a boy like Tony without understanding him? Les also tells me that some people are scared to let their kids play with poor kids because 'they think the poverty will rub off on them'. I don't think it is necessarily the poverty so much as what we associate with it: ruthlessness, lawlessness, unpredictability.

Conservatism speaks of generational wisdom being passed down, but when the only chronicle of life you have received comes day-to-day on an ad hoc basis, depending on how high or low your parents are, whether they've scored or how much they've gambled away, then you have to create your own story. When these kids turn on the telly or read the papers, the only future they see for themselves is the thug's life: riots at the Parkville detention centre, Don Dale, the Apex gang. We are not interested in the true stories of former child soldiers in the housing commission flats down the road, or the South-East Asian kids of my youth who came here as unaccompanied minors, got in with the wrong crowds and onto drugs. We say there is no innocence in these young terrors, but by that we mean there is nothing 'childlike' about them. They do not match our perception of what children or young adults should be. They know *too much*, their experience is *too much*, even for us adults.

Maybe that's where the real problem lies. Our egos get in the way of imaginative empathy; our own fears taint the truth. When Helen Garner wrote about the drowning of three young boys, she irately observed, 'People seem more prepared to contemplate a book about a story as dark as this if the writer comes galloping out with all moral guns blazing.' Susan Sontag wrote in *Regarding the Pain of Others*: 'Someone who is permanently surprised that depravity exists, who continues to feel disillusioned (even incredulous) when confronted with evidence of what humans are capable of inflicting in the way of gruesome, hands-on cruelties upon other humans, has not reached moral or psychological adulthood.'

Early in your teaching career, John, you took a class of students to an abattoir after they were bored reading *Bless the Beasts and Children*. You mentioned that one of the most powerful scenes you've ever encountered about death was Maxim Gorky's visceral account of Tsiganok's last hours in *My Childhood*. You were also quite staggered that readers didn't recognise a death scene in one of your own books: 'In describing Corrie's condition in the hospital, I thought I had given a strong enough hint that she was dying, and I was a bit surprised by the number of readers who asked about her in subsequent months.'

Children's lack of exposure to death, suffering and general unpleasantness means that they cannot recognise its occurrence in literature, despite clear signs. An inability to confront any sort of violence is now correlated with virtue. I remember the horror and awe my Vietnamese friend's four-year-old son inspired in a girl twice his age because he was carrying around a green-and-yellow water pistol in a park. 'Mum, that boy's got a gun! A GUN!' she dobbed, tugging her mother's sleeve. We call this reaction innocence and consider it a desirable trait. Yet left unchecked, as an adult it can transmute into something uglier – a lack of empathy, a rigid assertion that the world and others must be a certain way to be deemed 'moral'.

By dint of this unassailable vision which sees the world in terms of good and evil, some kids are considered bad influences because they are 'damaged'. There are a lot of 'damaged' kids in your books, John, and you don't provide happy endings for them. Tony is still full of apoplectic rage at the conclusion of *Dear Miffy*. Tracey sinks deeper into the abyss at the end of *Letters from the Inside*. Lisa from *Take My Word For It* reveals a suicide attempt. These kids have really been messed up by life, and they're barely sixteen. We forget how little actual power they have – they can't drive, they can't vote, they have legal guardians.

When you started writing *Tomorrow, When the War Began*, you saw the book as an opportunity to counter the prevailing, often unquestioned, lazy narrative about dangerous adolescents: 'According to the popular media, every teenager in Australia is either illiterate, drug-crazed, suicidal, alcoholic, criminal, promiscuous, selfish, a dole bludger or all of the above.'

The idea that 'good' children can be corrupted by literary representations of 'bad' or 'criminal' children is a real problem, particularly when these 'good' children are the ones our society trains to be future leaders. A person can reach a certain level of comfort and complacency in life where the troubles of others – mental illness, poverty, neglect – seem as though they have simple solutions. Perhaps they do – in stability, love, faith. But, as your books demonstrate, these gifts are not guaranteed for every child or young adult, and the path to obtaining them isn't easy. Some kids aren't even on the path; they're still at the side of the road, thumb out in doleful hope:

> Life seems so fragile. You walk down the centre of the highway, with the big trucks rushing past. They make the air shake. They blow you off your line. You stick out your arms to get your balance. A truck hits one arm and spins you around. You stagger

and fall, holding your arm and crying. Another truck rushes at you. There's no escape. Your body's just bones and flesh, that's all. There are too many things beating at you, blowing at you, hurting you and leaving bruises.

Adolescence is the time when young people are statistically most likely to come into harm's way, and thus more likely to witness harm among their peers. It is also the time when they are most likely to develop a mental illness, as Marina does in *So Much to Tell You*:

I seem to be dropping into a cold dark wet place, where no one's been before and no one can ever follow. There's no future there; just a past that sometimes fools you into thinking it's the future. It's the most alone place you can ever be and, when you go there, you not only cease to exist in real life, you also cease to exist in their consciousness and in their memories.

You've always honoured the truth, John. If you hadn't had the breakdown in your teens when you felt suicidally depressed, where the safest place you found was a psychiatric hospital, perhaps these truths would never have emerged. Your nameless narrator in *Checkers* says: 'in some ways this world [of the psychiatric hospital] is more real than the one outside. In here the masks are off, people don't pretend so much. We still fake it when we can, but most of the time we don't have the energy or the strength.'

If a person is psychologically healthy, well adjusted and well supported, reading about clinical depression isn't going to make them sick.

As a teenager I didn't understand the charges of hopelessness levelled at *Dear Miffy*. What a voice! Tony is funny, self-deprecating at times, even affectionate. Underlying all this is his blinding bull rage, the only sign of potency in his otherwise abject circumstances. I didn't find the book bleak because Tony was a) alive, and b) writing. I still don't find it bleak, since I know plenty of young men who are neither, who lost that battle.

Yes, John, 'It's a miracle anyone survives to be a teenager. It's a miracle any teenager survives to be an adult.'

I n literature, as in life, a child has to wrest the narrative power away from the grown-ups to reach adulthood. Children have to come to the realisation that they are grown-up themselves. This is probably not going to happen in real life if self-appointed 'gatekeepers' of YA literature insist on a mandatory quota of at least 2.5 responsible, supervisory adult characters in each novel! A friend, Margaret, who, as I observed, has a particularly special and close relationship of mutual respect with her teenage daughter, told me that parents could choose whatever parenting strategy they wanted, but they had to understand the consequences: if you decide to use control as the primary mode of interacting with your child, she said, you should also remember that in a very short time that child is going to be physically bigger than you, smarter than you, stronger than you – and their physical and worldly prowess will only increase, while yours will not.

In your books, John, an adult's capacity to graciously concede power at the right time makes all the difference to the teenager's journey. The New Zealand army commanders allowed Ellie and her friends to go back into the war zone, and trusted their judgement. Mr Murlin gives his Year 5 class freedom, but still maintains responsibility: "'although we're all important in here, there are a few jobs that are especially mine'", he tells the students. "'And discipline's one of them. So I'll take care of that.'"

But when irrational, selfish or benighted adults force their decisions upon intelligent teenagers, characters like Tony, Miffy and Tracey seize power in any way they can, while Marina is so oppressed that she loses her ability to speak. These 'damaged' children have never felt like narrators of their own lives, and their struggle is to gain agency over their stories – Tracey through her lies, Tony and Miffy through their wild behaviour, and Marina through her silence.

When there is no longer a relationship of mutual respect, young adults feel compelled to crush their parents. As Winter observes of her peers: 'Daughters kill their mothers in all kinds of ways. If not when they're giving birth, then later. Some of my friends in Canberra were killing their mothers slowly, one day at a time, death by a million cuts.'

After her dad bashes a photographer, the narrator of *Checkers* feels pity, but also a sense of potency for the first time: 'Dad stood there without moving. His head was down. I felt sorry for him, but I felt sort of masterful, in control … He followed me into the house and I got him a whisky.' By this stage the father is a pathetic man, whose integrity the narrator has always doubted. In contrast, Emine, a Turkish girl at the psychiatric institution, is deeply reluctant to speak ill of her parents. Accordingly, she suffers under the narrative weight of their infallibility and judgement. When her father catches her on the phone with a boy, he circumscribes her life so much that she has a breakdown, which brings more shame on her family.

Virginia Woolf once said that it is more difficult to murder a phantom than a reality. Tony's selfish, lying, abusive dad is a far cry from the idealised father in his mind, while he still holds out hope, against all reason, for his mother's return: 'I sort of think she'll be able to fix everything up for me somehow, wave some fucking wand.' Fighting a set of overbearing parents may be difficult enough, but fighting *indifferent* parents is virtually impossible.

One of the biggest complaints about your books is that adult characters aren't given much faith or credit for being kind, understanding or helpful. But I can think of plenty of examples, in every book: Homer's parents, Mr Lindell, Mr Hammond, the counsellors at the psychiatric hospital in *Checkers*, the prison warder Miss Gruber in *Letters from the Inside*, not to mention all the adults who help Ellie and her friends through the war. Your adult characters, like your children and teenagers, are as nuanced and diverse as adults I know in real life: frightened victims, generous assisters, petty gossips, sleazy powerbrokers, selfless friends, insecure parents, inspiring teachers and everything in between. The only thing they don't do – which perhaps well-adjusted and powerful adults feel they should – is charge in and 'save the day'.

Yet none of your novels is simply about children or teenagers 'showing up' adults either, making them look like fools, or teaching the 'grown-ups' a lesson. In fact, you are equally disgusted by mawkish portrayals of children in movies: children who bring sparring adults together, forcing them to give precedence to 'family over work' and other handy life lessons that can be imparted in two hours of screen-time.

Your most potent metaphor for an adolescent finding their voice and agency is the *Tomorrow* series, where teenagers learn to survive from day to day, in a realistic world devoid of adult supervision. Because he is always getting into trouble at school, it is only in war that Homer gets to make his own decisions and do practical things, revealing his leadership skills and high intelligence. Lee, who'd always been a mysterious peripheral character, becomes central to the survival of the group when the battles begin. Robyn, from a stable, loving, Christian household, learns to live up to her convictions in a devastatingly heroic way. At the beginning of the series, these characters were minors who had to get their parents' permission to go camping for a couple of days. By the end, they are war legends. But the true path to maturity for Ellie Linton and her friends is to realise that adults are fallible, and to come to some sort of acceptance, forgiveness and responsibility.

'Old people are wise,' one young adult writer said on our panel at Melbourne Writers Festival a few years ago. He was in his twenties, a charming young man trying earnestly to be a Good Role Model.

'No, that's not true,' you interrupted. 'Just because a person is old doesn't mean they necessarily gain any wisdom.' You repeated what you wrote in *Secret Men's Business*, that chronological age didn't mean anything: 'I've known people of 12 who are well-balanced, intelligent, thoughtful, empathetic. I've known people of 60 who are spiteful, selfish, prejudiced, shallow.'

You see maturity and morality as a tautology. You once said, 'I consider it a disturbing aspect of our culture that most young people can become adults merely by staying alive and having birthdays.' It is the very idea of human social responsibility, and not vague notions of humanity, that drives your work as a writer and a teacher; specific actions rather than sweeping grandiose ideas. Action upon action, your characters build experience. Ellie Linton realises that:

> Life's about a hell of a lot more than being happy. It's about feeling the full range of stuff: happiness, sadness, anger, grief, love, hate. If you try to shut one of those off, you shut them all off. I don't want to be happy. I know I won't live happily ever after. I want more than that, something richer. I want to go right up close to the beauty and the ugliness. I want to see it all, know it all, understand it all.

The richness and the poverty, the joy and the cruelty, the sweetness and the sadness. That's the best way I can honour my friends who died.

As the principal of two schools now, you have an educational philosophy congruent with your writing philosophy, a hard-won vision of accepting joy and suffering with equanimity:

There is a Korean saying that life is 10,000 joys, 10,000 sorrows. And so to graduate children who are able to cope with the 10,000 sorrows that they'll inevitably encounter, and are able to totally experience and enjoy the 10,000 joys, that's the aim of education – producing happy children or neat children or well-mannered children is nothing compared to that.

This reminds me of a Buddhist monk, Ajahn Chah, who once said that we are always trying to find a good person, or be a good person: 'We should do good for the sake of goodness, not in order to become a "good person". If we are a "good person" then we will suffer. Just be a human being. Otherwise we will always be annoyed by those who are not "good people".'

The most satisfying young adult literature I have read has always been built on the premise that there are no 'good' or 'bad' people, only the negative or positive consequences of one's own actions:

What's all this 'should' and 'supposed to' stuff? We're talking about people here, human beings ... Once you start to formulate codes of behaviour and decide that everyone has to abide by them, and that those who don't are rude or ignorant or bad, then you've lost sight of what people are.

This is why I've always admired your work. There are no easy or simple answers, and the teaching and the writing is deeply moral. In *Secret Men's Business*, you tell young men that: 'you can do anything you want, as long as you accept the consequences'. This philosophy allows the teenagers in *The Ellie Chronicles* to survive the war with their essential moral selves intact. You also advise young men that, 'Cynicism is like gastro: it goes through your whole system and makes you shitty.' Cynicism is not the same as accepting that bad things happen in life; and the false optimism adults sometimes give children is the worst form of cynicism, because it is a lie premised on an utter lack of faith in a young person's judgement.

You see individual human development – social, philosophical, physical – as part of a continuum; therefore, there is no need to fear a child's transition into independence and psychological maturity. You would feel proud if children could pick up adult narratives and examine them closely for holes, because only through the holes can we see the light. Yet adults still like to create watertight storylines in junior and young adult literature, in the belief that the less permeable a story, the better it can hold the weighty message being impressed upon those 'impressionable' minds. Yes, we may block out all the holes, but we also block out all the light.

Argus becomes a man when he can tell stories of his own that assimilate the duality of darkness and light, and one of his stories is about learning to accept darkness but keep it at bay: 'It was then, with her new understanding, that

Alzire became aware this creature could never be killed, but only kept as small as possible, and stopped from growing. To keep it so small as to be insignificant was perhaps the greatest and most important task that life offered.'

Similarly, the character you say you most identify with in the *Tomorrow* series, Chris Lang, writes: 'I live in the light, / But carry my dark with me.'

A young adult has to spend some time in the dark to have sharper vision: to see shapes outlined more clearly, to avoid bumping into hazards. Left to her own devices, sixteen-year-old Ellie discovers something that many people never realise in their lifetimes:

> People just stick ... names on places, so that no one could see those places properly anymore. Every time they looked at them

or thought about them the first thing they saw was a huge big sign saying 'Housing Commission' or 'private school' or 'church' or 'mosque' or 'synagogue'. They stopped looking once they saw those signs.

Ellie learns to see.

When my son was born, he was very small, barely over two kilos, yet when I looked at him in his humidicrib I recognised with awe how complete he was as a human being, a separate entity from me. I spent hours just staring at him when we came home, aware that this was the first time in my life I could look so directly at another person without feeling self-conscious, because he did not yet have a sense of self and his eyes were still unfocused. Friends asked me, 'Is he a good baby?' and I always said yes, but actually I could not think about him in those terms. I did not consider him a good or a bad baby. He was just a baby. It was like asking if a lion was a good or a bad lion. I understood the thrust of the question (is he a bother to us, or does he create bliss in our lives?), but I didn't think the purpose of his existence was to bend to our whims.

I realised what complete power my husband, Nick, and I had over him, physically and verbally. For over a year I watched this human being come into consciousness and self-awareness – first crying, then pointing, then single words, and later full sentences. With each development, we became more aware of the burgeoning complexity of his needs – preferences he can now vocalise (blueberry over banana), experiences he tells us he remembers, and a growing determined independence ('Do by self!' is his favourite expression, which he hollers even in his sleep).

Even before he could speak, he always listened carefully when I recounted his exploits to his dad at the end of each day. But I wondered, do I give faithful accounts? What do I give importance to in my telling of his story? And now that he is beginning to talk, what sorts of things will he trust to tell us? When he is a teenager, what might he feel compelled to hide because our version of him is inconsistent with his truth?

I recently read about a Harvard study in which parents were asked what they wanted for their children, and the parents invariably gave a high priority to kindness. However, 80 per cent of the youth surveyed said their parents were more concerned with their achievements or happiness than whether they cared for others. This response seems unsurprising since human beings can generally detect when words are inconsistent with actions, and most popular literature about Western parenting focuses on the success or happiness generated by the enterprise (replete with words like 'rewarding', 'treasure' and even 'investment').

Yet we expect children's literature to shape our kids into good, kind people, and get angry when these books fail to live up to our didactic expectations! But I think of you, John, whenever I let my son play with toy guns, when I buy him clothes with many little pockets ('There may be a deep Freudian reason for this. If so, I don't know it. All I know is, the more pockets the better.'), and when we teach him to cook. You reassure boys that there is nothing wrong with them if they don't like reading, since they probably have other hobbies. I trust your judgement and experience, mainly because you say things like this:

I think it's really dangerous if you write a book, to believe that you have some understanding of the world that other people don't have. You have some exclusive access to the truth and you're going to very kindly write this novel and let other people share your wonderful exclusive knowledge. I use books to explore things I don't understand.

And you also give excellent parenting advice:

One of the greatest gifts you can give your son is to help him understand that he will always have greedy, angry, lustful, selfish and lazy feelings, and a lot more besides. And there will be plenty of times when he will act out these feelings. Our aim as humans should be to incorporate these aspects in a way that causes minimal damage to ourselves and others, and also to continue to develop our generous, wise, hardworking, honest and compassionate aspects.

Newspapers hail you as 'Australia's King of Young Adult Fiction' because you've sold millions of books; but I reckon you're the king because in all your writing, it's as if you are on your knees, eye-level and ear-level with your child subjects, humbling yourself before them to see what they see and hear what they hear.

ell, we're near the end now, John. I have to say, it's probably easier to write about dead people you admire than living ones, particularly ones who have already written two books on their own writing process. You've been interviewed on television, radio and newspapers by every major journalist, and some guy in America has even written a book about your work. When an interviewer asked what you would be if you were an amusement-park ride and why, you replied, 'Well, I'm a bit bruised by life, so I'd be something that people chuck things at.' Flaubert once wrote, 'Never touch your idols. The gilt will stick to your fingers.' I didn't imagine I would ever meet you, let alone that you would launch one of my books, or that we would become friends.

We first met at the Brisbane Writers Festival — my first festival as an author — when you were signing books. You signed my *Hamlet*. You once said that, 'Most of our definitions of success involve being loved by strangers, which is a meaningless concept, because strangers can't love someone because they can't know them.' But I already adored you then, because I stood back and watched you talk to each child and young adult rather than the publicists and parents milling around. In fact, if parents were taking up too much time with meandering anecdotes, you cut them short.

You carry Ernest Hemingway's essential attribute for an author, 'a built-in bullshit detector.' There was definitely no gilt stuck on you that day that would disappear with the first downpour, but I think I already knew this. I didn't introduce myself then because that first encounter for me was like meeting the Queen. I also thought it would be too presumptuous, as I believed that I would peter out as a writer, a one-shot wonder. But you would always be there. You signed my book, 'Take care, Take risks.' I saw those pale blue eyes, which have the kindness of Robin Williams and the wildness of Gustav Klimt, and thought, *This is the pinnacle of my writing career!*

The next time I saw you was at your talk at Victoria University. You were recently married and a stepfather to six boys. Your interviewer, the boisterous Bruno Lettieri, asked the audience to cheer for your good news and happily embarrassed you. You gave away copies of your book *Marsden on Marsden,* displaying the same kindness you showed my friend Angela all those years ago when her mum bumped into your car.

You talked about your school Candlebark, and your contempt for a teacher who kept referring to the students as 'kiddies'. During the break, you ate a sandwich in the corner, quiet and self-contained as a wombat in a brown woolly jumper. I didn't disturb you then either, but you no longer seemed like a legend and more like a living, breathing human being who was a bit tired and probably wanted to get home to his new family.

Over the years, we've been at other writing and school events together. Usually, you'd be the one giving the keynote address, ad-libbing about creativity and bending the rules, and always bringing down the house. We'd exchange greetings and talk a bit in green rooms.

Then you agreed to launch my book at Janet Clarke Hall.

Although your leg was in a cast, you drove all the way to the city from your home in Romsey.

You had ordered a chocolate champagne bottle for the launch, but it melted in your car. You said, 'Fuck you' during your speech, in an anecdote about an exchange between a teacher and a student (the student was not the one who needed to wash his mouth out with soap). My mum wanted to know how you broke your leg; my dad wanted to know how you'd sold so many books; and all my sisters, cousins and students crowded around you.

Two years ago, I unexpectedly received an email from you after we saw each other at the Bendigo Writers Festival, after a devastating tragedy in my life. It gave me more comfort than you will ever realise, because you did not offer false consolation. I think our friendship was cemented then.

The other day, I found a newspaper article from three years ago that my father had kept. It was about your first adult book, *South of Darkness,* but I think he kept it because in it you talked about your lifetime of battling mental illness. You grew up in the 1950s when men just didn't talk about their true feelings, and I grew up in a house where we didn't talk much about them either. (How could any of our trivial laments compare to surviving genocide or burying loved ones?)

I know that having depression means never having a firm grasp of an essential self that some people take for granted. You wrote in *Checkers* that, 'People talk about thick skin and thin skin, but we don't have any.' Nothing is certain; nothing is permanent. But then again, a complete erosion of ego is perhaps a good thing. Buddhists certainly believe so. When you have no ego, you are more open and permeable to the world.

In my late teens and early twenties, I resigned myself to the idea that I would be working and saving up all my life to tide me over the times I might break down. When I went through the worst grief I'd ever experienced two years ago, I envied those who had God, and certainty, and an unassailable sense of self. I wanted to cling to anything and everything that might keep me afloat. I received this email from you during that time:

> I was trying to figure out this morning, in a vague existential sort of way, why we attach so much importance to our lives when, without a religious belief, it's hard to know why they have any value or purpose or meaning. Needless to say I couldn't come up with any answers :-).

That smiley face made my day.

A certain type of reader might feel they are owed a happy ending. But you can't please everyone. Many people were deeply disappointed by how you ended the *Tomorrow* series. The reviews on Goodreads kept stacking up, going on and on about how Homer and Ellie would have been perfect together because they could have merged farms and brought up Gavin.

But the fact that Ellie the brave, the light, the survivor, ends up with Lee the dark, the brooding, the depressed, the teenager stuck in a flat with all those siblings to support, was a triumph to me. Lee's quest to do the right thing throughout the series is made all the more difficult by a lack of any external recognition or support: he is the first to lose his parents, and even his mates start jokingly calling him a 'killing machine'. He doesn't say much, and he's not charming like Homer or Jeremy Finley or even Jay Gatenby.

Yet in Lee, I recognised parts of myself as well as all the kids I grew up with – those quiet teenagers with adult responsibilities and overprotective, war-traumatised parents. For introverts, Asian males, teens battling mental illness, teens who feel 'damaged' by experience with no unconditional adult support to alleviate their burden, teens who can't believe they will ever be loved – this ending felt like a recognition of internal resilience, loyalty, and a dogged commitment to a vision of love as a verb, not an adjective. *You saw us.*

Love and deep respect,
From your friend,
Alice

SOURCES

3   '"Millie is an odious"': Posted by Louise (A Strong
     Belief in Wicker), *Goodreads*, 11 December 2011,
     www.goodreads.com/book/show/6325333-millie

4   'you don't include the punishment at the end': Lynley
     Stace, 'Picturebook study: *Millie* by John Marsden
     and Sally Rippin', *Slap Happy Larry*, 15 April 2015,
     www.slaphappylarry.com/picturebook-study-millie-
     by-john-marsden-and-sally-rippin/

5   'To have turned so many children': Belinda Hawkins
     and Kent Gordon (producers), 'Dear John', *Australian
     Story*, ABC TV, 9 September 2002. Transcript
     available at www.abc.net.au/austory/transcripts/
     s667721.htm

6   'If you've ever tried': John Marsden, *Secret Men's
     Business*, Pan Macmillan, Sydney, 1998, p. 75.

6   'plenty of adults are impressionable': Ibid., pp. 48–49.

7   'In 1992, Susan Orlean wrote': Susan Orlean, 'The
     American Male at Age Ten', *Esquire*, December 1992.

7   "'If Colin Duffy and I were to get married"': Ibid.

8   "'That ten-year-olds feel"': Ibid.

8   "'Colin loves recycling"': Ibid.

8–9   'I was struck': John Marsden, *Marsden on Marsden: The Stories Behind John Marsden's Bestselling Books*, Pan Macmillan, Sydney, 2000, p. 65.

10   'My first day I sat next to': John Marsden, *The Year My Life Broke*, Pan Macmillan, Sydney, 2013, p. 10.

11   'I really grew to adore this kid': John Boe, 'An Interview with Susan Orlean: "The Nature of the Curious Mind"', *Writing on the Edge*, Issue 15, Volume 2, University of California at Davis, California, 2005, pp. 92–108.

12   'tragic reports about garage-sewing': Christina Cregan, 'Tales of Despair: Outworker Narratives', Department of Management, University of Melbourne, 22 November 2001.

12   'Until adolescence, parents by and large': Rachel Cusk, 'Raising Teenagers: The Mother of All Problems', *The New York Times Magazine*, 19 March 2015.

13   '[It made] me realise that my non-romantic way': Posted by Rusalka, *Goodreads*, 7 December 2012, www.goodreads.com/book/show/82614.Dear_Miffy

17   "'the twin fortresses"': Cusk, 'Raising Teenagers'.

19   'first experiences can push you': Marsden, *Secret Men's Business*, p. 77.

19   'I wonder how much': Cusk, 'Raising Teenagers'.

20   'telling lies to anyone is wrong': Marsden, *Secret Men's Business*, p. 41.

20   'go to prison': John Marsden, *Dear Miffy*, Pan Macmillan, Sydney, 1997.

20   'mental institutions': Marsden, *Dear Miffy*; John Marsden, *Checkers*, Houghton Mifflin, Boston, 1998.

20   'war': John Marsden, *Tomorrow, When the War Began*, Pan Macmillan, Sydney, 1993. See also the subsequent books in the series (listed in bibliography).

20   'have sex': John Marsden, *The Great Gatenby*, Pan Macmillan, Sydney, 1989; John Marsden, *The Journey*, Pan Macmillan, Sydney, 1990; John Marsden, *The Dead of the Night*, Pan Macmillan, Sydney, 1994; Marsden, *Dear Miffy*.

20   'run their deceased parents' estates': John Marsden, *Winter*, Pan Macmillan, Sydney, 2000.

20   'inadvertently get caught up in political scandals': Marsden, *Checkers*.

20   'experience domestic violence': John Marsden, *Letters from the Inside*, Pan Macmillan, Sydney, 1991.

20   'rob, assault and kill': Marsden, *Tomorrow, When the War Began*, and subsequent books in the series.

20   'rendering them wordless': John Marsden, *So Much to Tell You*, Walter McVitty Books, Glebe, 1987.

23   "'I think we're going to end up with'": Interview with Andrew Denton, *Enough Rope*, ABC TV, 21 June 2004. Transcript available at www.abc.net.au/tv/enoughrope/transcripts/s1137536.htm

24   "'At home they drove vehicles'": Marsden, *Marsden on Marsden*, p. 76.

25   "'If the bull had wanted'": John Marsden, *Circle of Flight*, Pan Macmillan, Sydney, 2006.

26   'Influenced by Hermann Hesse's *Siddhartha*': Marsden, *Marsden on Marsden*, p. 39.

27   "'It suddenly struck him'": Marsden, *The Journey*, p. 124.

27   'Aung San Suu Kyi said that': Aung San Suu Kyi, *Freedom from Fear*, Penguin, London, 1995.

28   "'[My mother] was so obviously a powerful personality'": Marsden, *Winter*, p. 116.

29   "'Mrs Neumann snapped'": Marsden, *Letters from the Inside*, p. 141.

29   'your week in Risdon Prison': Marsden, *Marsden on Marsden*, p. 57.

30   'a line from Ecclesiastes': Ecclesiastes, 4:1, *Bible New International Version*.

30   "'I love it how they call it'": Marsden, *Dear Miffy*, p. 2.

31   "'the subculture of some young men and women'": Marsden, *Marsden on Marsden*, p. 113.

33   "'People seem more prepared'": Helen Garner, 'The Darkness in Every One of Us', *The Monthly*, July 2015.

33   'Susan Sontag wrote': Susan Sontag, *Regarding the Pain of Others*, Penguin, 2001, p. 103.

34   'Early in your teaching career': Claire Forster, Belinda Hawkins and Kent Gordon (producers), 'The School that John Built', *Australian Story*, ABC TV, 18 September 2007. Transcript available at: www.abc.net.au/austory/content/2007/s2036865.htm

34   'one of the most powerful scenes': Marsden, *Secret Men's Business*, p. 54–55.

34   "'In describing Corrie's condition'": Marsden, *Marsden on Marsden*, p. 83.

36   "'According to the popular media'": Ibid., p. 70.

37–38   "'Life seems so fragile'": Marsden, *Checkers*, p. 12.

38   'most likely to come into harm's way': In 2015, suicide was the leading cause of death for both males and females aged between fifteen and twenty-four: Australian Institute of Health and Welfare, *Deaths Data*, accessed 23 March 2017: www.aihw.gov.au/deaths/

38   'most likely to develop a mental illness': Jay Giedd,
      Matcheri Keshavan and Tomas Paus, 'Why Do
      So Many Psychiatric Disorders Emerge During
      Adolesence?', *National Review of Neuroscience*, Issue
      12, Volume 9, December 2008, pp. 947–957.

38–39 "'I seem to be dropping'": Marsden, *So Much to Tell
      You*, p. 87.

39   "'in some ways this world'": Marsden, *Checkers*, p. 52.

40   "'It's a miracle anyone survives'": Ibid., p. 12.

42   "'although we're all important in here'": John
      Marsden, *Staying Alive in Year 5*, Pan Macmillan,
      Sydney, 1996, p. 6–7.

43   "'Daughters kill their mothers'": Marsden, *Winter*,
      p. 129.

43–44 "'Dad stood there without moving'": Marsden,
      Checkers, p. 70.

44   'Virginia Woolf once said': Virginia Woolf, *The
      Death of the Moth and Other Essays*, Mariner Books,
      New York, 1974.

44–45 "'I sort of think she'll be able to fix everything up'":
      Marsden, *Dear Miffy*, p. 98.

48   "'I've known people of 12'": Marsden, *Secret Men's
      Business*, p. 44.

48–49 "'I consider it a disturbing aspect'": Marsden,
      Marsden on Marsden, p. 38.

49–50 "'Life's about a hell of a lot more'": John Marsden, *The Other Side of Dawn*, Pan Macmillan, Sydney, 1999.

50 "'There is a Korean saying'": Claire Forster, Belinda Hawkins and Kent Gordon (producers), 'The School that John Built'.

51 'This reminds me of a Buddhist monk': Ajahn Chah, Essence of Buddhism, essenceofbuddhism.wordpress.com/2014/07/25/ajahn-chah-on-doing-good-for-the-sake-of-goodness-not-to-become-a-good-person/.

51–52 "'What's all this 'should''": Marsden, *The Journey*, p. 68.

52 "'you can do anything you want'": Marsden, *Secret Men's Business*, p. 36.

52 "'Cynicism is like gastro'": Ibid., p. 41.

53–54 "'It was then, with her new understanding'": Marsden, *The Journey*, p. 142.

54 "'I live in the light'": Marsden, *The Dead of the Night*, p. 176.

54–55 "'People just stick …'": Marsden, *Tomorrow, When the War Began*, p. 43–44.

58 'I recently read about a Harvard study': Amy Joyce, 'Are You Raising Nice Kids? A Harvard Psychologist Gives 5 Ways To Raise Them To Be Kind', *The*

Washington Post, 18 July 2014, www.washingtonpost.
com/news/parenting/wp/2014/07/18/
are-you-raising-nice-kids-a-harvard-psychologist-
gives-5-ways-to-raise-them-to-be-kind/?utm_term=.
f43402dc7d68

59   'whenever I let my son play with toy guns': John
      Marsden, *The Boy You Brought Home: A Single
      Mother's Guide to Raising Sons*, Pan Macmillan,
      Sydney, 2002, p. 7.

59   'when I buy him clothes with many little pockets':
      Ibid., p. 25.

59   'when we teach him to cook': Ibid., p. 9.

59   'You reassure boys that': Ibid., p. 38.

59–60 '"I think it's really dangerous"': Interview with
      George Negus, *George Negus Tonight Profiles*, ABC
      TV, 4 November 2004. Transcript available at: www.
      abc.net.au/gnt/profiles/Transcripts/s1235463.htm.

60–61 '"One of the greatest gifts"': Marsden, *The Boy You
      Brought Home*, p. 86.

62   'already written two books on their own writing
      process': John Marsden, *Everything I Know About
      Writing*, Pan Macmillan Australia, Sydney, 1993;
      Marsden, *Marsden on Marsden*.

62   'some guy in America has even written a book
      about your work': John Noell Moore, *John Marsden:*

Darkness, Shadow and Light, Studies in Young Adult Literature, Book 40, Scarecrow Press, Lanham, Maryland, 2010.

62 "'Well, I'm a bit bruised by life'": ABC Rollercoaster, 'Interview with John Marsden', *The Rap*, ABC TV, accessed 24 March 2017: www.abc.net.au/rollercoaster/therap/interviews/s1532838.htm

67 "'People talk about thick skin'": Marsden, *Checkers*, p. 67.

BOOKS BY JOHN MARSDEN

THE *TOMORROW* SERIES

Tomorrow, When the War Began (1993)

The Dead of the Night (1994)

The Third Day, the Frost (1995)

Darkness, Be My Friend (1996)

Burning for Revenge (1997)

The Night is for Hunting (1998)

The Other Side of Dawn (1999)

THE ELLIE CHRONICLES

While I Live (2003)

Incurable (2005)

Circle of Flight (2006)

OTHER WORKS

So Much to Tell You (1987)

The Journey (1988)

The Great Gatenby (1989)

Staying Alive in Year 5 (1990)

Out of Time (1990)

Letters from the Inside (1991)

Take My Word for It (1992)

Looking for Trouble (1993)

Everything I Know About Writing (1993)

Cool School (1996)

Creep Street (1996)

Checkers (1996)

This I Believe (ed.) (1996)

For Weddings and a Funeral (ed.) (1996)

Dear Miffy (1997)

Prayer for the Twenty-First Century (1997)

Norton's Hut (illustrated by Peter Gouldthorpe) (1998)

The Rabbits (illustrated by Shaun Tan) (1998)

Secret Men's Business (1998)

Winter (2000)

Marsden on Marsden (2000)

The Head Book (2001)

Millie (illustrated by Sally Rippin) (2002)

The Magic Rainforest (2002)

A Day in the Life of Me (illustrated by Craig Smith) (2002)

The Boy You Brought Home (2002)

A Roomful of Magic (illustrated by Mark Jackson and Heather Potter) (2004)

Hamlet: A Novel (2008)

Home and Away (illustrated by Matt Ottley) (2008)

South of Darkness (2014)